Near
Water

Ruth Thomson

Commissioned photography by
Chris Fairclough

W
FRANKLIN WATTS
LONDON • SYDNEY

© 2004 Franklin Watts

First published in 2004 by
Franklin Watts
96 Leonard Street
London
EC2A 4XD

Franklin Watts Australia
45-51 Huntley Street
Alexandria
NSW 2015

ISBN: 0 7496 5469 4

A CIP catalogue record for this book is available from the British Library

Printed in Malaysia
Planning and production by Discovery Books Limited
Editor: Helena Attlee
Designer: Ian Winton
Consultants: Alison Curtis, Manager of Streetwise Safety Centre,
Bournemouth and Steve Wills, Beach Safety Officer, RNLI.

The author, packager and publisher would like to thank the following people for their
participation in this book: Richard, Diane, Oliver and Thomas Newton; David Hills,
Darren Lewis, Alex Hill and Ollie Rogers of the RNLI; Lydia and Milton Hamilton;
Rachel and Karen Sheffield; Helen Bromley and Sharon Burns.

Contents

At the swimming pool   4

Fun in the pool   6

Waterplay in the garden   8

Rivers and canals   10

Down by the river   12

The sunny seaside   14

On the beach   16

Waves and tides   18

Cliffs and rockpools   20

Swimming in the sea   22

Danger at sea   24

To the rescue   26

At the harbour   28

Glossary   30

Useful addresses and websites   31

Index   32

At the swimming pool

The summer holidays have begun and the weather is baking hot. Mum has taken Thomas, Oliver and Rachel to the swimming pool. The children cannot wait to get in the water. Mum and Rachel step into the small, shallow pool.

Don't run!

Thomas and Oliver start running towards the big pool. The lifeguard blows his whistle to stop them. 'Don't run!' he shouts. 'You might slip on the wet tiles and hurt yourselves, or even fall into the water!'

Thomas walks to the deep end and gets ready to dive in.

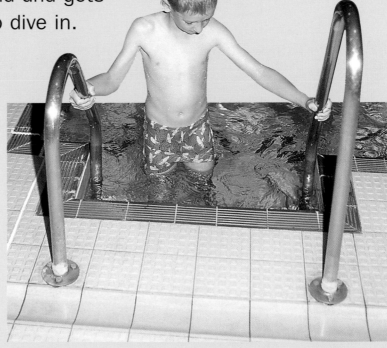

Oliver cannot swim as well as Thomas. He goes to the shallow end and climbs down the pool steps.

Swimming pool safety rules

- Don't run along the pool edge.
- Don't dive into the shallow end.
  - Look before you dive.
  - Listen to the lifeguard, who is there to help you.
  - Never go into a pool if you're the only person there.
  - If you're not a good swimmer, never go into deep water.

SHALLOW END

NO

DIVING

IN THE SHALLOW END

FERNDOWN LEISURE CENTRE

Fun in the pool

Oliver holds on to a float and practises the kicks he has learnt in his swimming lessons. Thomas practises his breaststroke.

'Let's see how many lengths we can swim,' suggests Thomas. 'I want to try for my 400-metre badge soon.'

SAFETY FACTS

Swimming badges

It is important for everybody to learn to swim. Most pools run swimming and lifesaving classes. You get a badge to sew on to your swimwear when you pass a test.

Learning to swim

Rachel cannot swim properly yet, so she wears armbands to keep her afloat. She holds Mum's hands so that she feels safe while she practises.

Slides

Some swimming pools have slides. Remember to go down a slide face up and feet first. Do not wear any jewellery – it might get caught, and then you could hurt yourself.

SAFETY FACTS

Swimming pool rescue

Lifeguards make sure that swimmers behave safely. They do not allow children to push anyone in, or push anyone under the water. If someone is in trouble, they use ropes, poles and floats to help them out.

Waterplay in the garden

It is so hot that the children decide to play with water in the afternoon as well. The boys have fun on the lawn. They spray each other with the garden hose and throw buckets of water.

Paddling pools

Mum blows up the paddling pool for Rachel to play in. She stays with Rachel the whole time: it is never safe to leave young children alone, even in shallow water.

Garden ponds

At tea-time, they go to Grandpa's house and meet their cousins. All the grandchildren like looking at the fish in his pond.

Grandpa has put a fence around the pond, to stop young children falling in and drowning.

Bath time

At the end of the day, Mum runs Rachel a warm bath. 'What a watery day you've had,' she says, as she helps Rachel to wash.

SAFETY FACTS

Young children should never be left in the bath on their own – even for a moment.

Rivers and canals

The next day, the family go for a walk by the river. Rushes and dense waterplants line the bank. The family take care not to walk too near to the edge, where the bank might be steep and could crumble away under their feet.

SAFETY FACTS

Canals

Be careful not to go near the edge of a canal, as it may be slippery. Make sure you stand well back to watch a lock open and close. When the water rushes in it becomes deep very quickly.

Weirs

'Can we swim here?' asks Thomas.
'Not a good idea,' says Dad, pointing at a weir. 'It's not safe to swim where water is moving as fast as that.'

SAFETY FACTS

Many watery places are not safe for swimming. Water in lakes, reservoirs and quarries is always too cold and often too deep as well. In winter, the water may be covered with ice. Never walk on ice. It might not be strong enough to hold your weight.

Down by the river

The children follow a path to the river's edge. Tiny fish are darting about in the shallow water. The children wade over the shingle in their waterproof sandals and gently dip their nets into the water.

SAFETY FACTS

Kayaking on rivers

People who go kayaking always wear a life jacket and helmet in case their kayak tips over. They learn from an expert how to steer and to right the kayak if it turns over.

Swimming in rivers

On their way back to the car the family cross a bridge. Now they can see how deep the river is.

'The water looks very cold!' Oliver shivers. 'But it looks clean,' says Thomas. 'It probably is cold,' says Dad. 'And even water that looks clean can have lots of germs and chemicals in it. That's why it's not a good idea to swim in rivers.'

SAFETY FACTS

Swimming in rivers

Some rivers have strong currents that are hard to swim against, and sometimes the water gets deep very suddenly. At the river, there are no lifeguards to help if you get into difficulties when swimming.

The sunny seaside

The following day, the family take a trip to the seaside. They take buckets, spades and towels with them. As they pass the lifeguard station on the promenade, they check the tides and the weather forecast.

Dad says, 'The beach is very crowded. If we get separated by mistake, let's meet here.'

BEACH SAFETY

FLAGS

SWIM ZONE

SURF CRAFT ZONE

DANGER - NO SWIMMING

FIND THE RED AND YELLOW FLAGS AND SWIM BETWEEN THEM

LOOK AT THE SAFETY SIGNS

ASK A LIFEGUARD FOR ADVICE

GET A FRIEND TO SWIM WITH YOU

STICK YOUR HAND UP AND SHOUT FOR HELP IF IN DIFFICULTY

LIFEGUARD SERVICE
10am - 6pm MAY - SEPT

BeachSafety

INFORMATION

Name of beach BRANKSOME CHINE
Date 13/08/03
Lifeguard(s) on duty 2
Weather SLIGHTLY HAZY / SUNNY
Air temp 22°
Water temp 21°
Wind direction NE - F/
Sea state SPRING TIDES
High tides 10:15 & 14:30
Low tides 17:30
Conditions CALM
Local information SLIP ON A TSHIRT!
+ DRINK LOTS OF WATER! SLAP ON A HAT!
SLOP ON SUNCREAM!

IF IN DOUBT, ASK A LIFEGUARD FOR ADVICE

BeachSafety

Playing in the sun

The family find a spot on the sand. They put up a beach tent to give themselves some shade.

'It's so hot,' says Mum, rubbing the children with sun cream. 'I think you should keep on your T-shirts and hats while you play.'

Safety in the sun

Spending time in hot sun can cause sunburn, so protect yourself. Remember:

- *SLIP on a T-shirt.*
- *SLOP on some sun cream (at least factor 25).*
- *SLAP on a hat.*

Try not to stay in direct sun between 11am and 3pm, as this is the hottest part of the day. Drink plenty of water all day long.

On the beach

Digging their sandcastle makes the children hungry, so they start eating their picnic.

'Can we go swimming after lunch?' asks Thomas.

'Not straight away,' says Dad. 'It's best to wait an hour or so after you've eaten, or you might get cramp. Let's go for a walk instead.'

Keep the beach clean

'Before you go,' says Mum, holding out a plastic bag, 'put all your rubbish in here to keep the beach tidy.'

Shells

The children make their way along the busy shore. 'Look what I've found!' calls Rachel, holding up a shell.
'I'll keep it safe for you,' says Dad. 'We will wash it in fresh water when we get home – or it will get really smelly.'

Beware of walking on shells or sharp objects that people have left on the beach. Wear non-slip beach shoes if you have them.

SAFETY FACTS

Try not to tread in dog mess. It can cause disease. There are often bins on promenades, so that dog owners can clear up after their dogs.

Clean Up After Your Dog
USE THIS BIN

Waves and tides

On their way, the children stop for a paddle.
'Does the sea ever stop moving?' asks Oliver.
'Never' replies Dad.

Waves

Waves are ripples made by wind blowing over the sea. Out at sea, waves rise and fall all the time. When waves reach land, they break with a crash or tumble with a soft splash.

Watching for waves

When it's windy, watch out for big waves. On steeply sloping beaches, waves can sometimes break with great force. They could knock you off your feet.

Talking about tides

Oliver notices a line of wet sand along the beach.

'That's where high tide has stopped,' says Dad. 'The tide rises up the beach and then goes out again. The place where it stops rising is called the tideline.'

SAFETY FACTS

Soft mudflats

Some places are very muddy when the tide goes out. The mud is so soft that if you walked there, you might sink right into it and get stuck.

Cliffs and rockpools

At the end of the beach a headland juts out into the sea. 'Can we go to those cliffs?' asks Oliver. 'I don't think Rachel can walk that far,' says Dad.

Cliffs

It is unsafe to walk near overhanging cliffs, in case of rockfalls. Never try climbing cliffs, as they are too steep and often crumbly.

DANGER
UNSAFE CLIFF PLEASE USE THE PATH DOWN TO THE BEACH →

Rock pools

'Let's go to the rock pools instead,' suggests Dad.
Some of the rocks near the pools are rough and covered
with sharp barnacles. Others are slippery with seaweed.

The children move very slowly, taking care where they put
their feet. They see other children busily looking for
shrimps and crabs.
'Can I see what you've caught?' Thomas asks one of them.

SAFETY FACTS

Watch the tide

**If you go clambering
along the rocks, keep
an eye on the sea.
Make sure your route
back will not be cut
off when the tide
comes in.**

Swimming in the sea

The family return from their walk. 'You can go swimming now,' Dad says to Thomas.
'The two red and yellow flags show the zone that the lifeguards patrol. That's the safest area to swim.'

Lifeguards

Thomas looks at the lifeguard. 'He'll have a good view of me from that chair,' he says.

SAFETY FACTS

Know your flags

Learn what the flags on the beach mean.

BEACH SAFETY

SWIM ZONE

SURF CRAFT ZONE

DANGER - NO SWIMMING

FLAGS

FIND THE RED AND YELLOW FLAGS AND SWIM BETWEEN THEM

LOOK AT THE SAFETY SIGNS

ASK A LIFEGUARD FOR ADVICE

GET A FRIEND TO SWIM WITH YOU

STICK YOUR HAND UP AND SHOUT FOR HELP IF IN DIFFICULTY

LIFEGUARD SERVICE
10am - 6pm MAY - SEPT

Lifeboats
BeachSafety
www.beachsafety.org.uk

Safe swimming

'We'll come and watch you, too,' says Mum.
'Don't forget to swim in line with the shore, not out
to sea,' says Dad. 'We won't move, so use us to
check your position.'
'Stay in your depth,'
suggests Mum, 'so you
can rest or walk out if
you get tired. Keep
checking you can touch
the bottom.'

SAFETY FACTS

Do NOT swim:

- alone.
- when you are tired.
- when you are cold.
- for too long.
- for an hour after meals.
- if a red flag is flying.
- if you feel unwell.
- in rough sea.
- if you have been out in the sun for a long time.
- near pipes, rocks, breakwaters or piers.

BRIGHTON PIER

It is dangerous & forbidden to jump, dive or swim from the pier.

Danger at sea

After his swim, Thomas is watching other bathers when he suddenly notices an inflatable that is being blown out to sea. There are two children holding it. Both of them are waving.

Inflatables

It's safest to play with inflatables in a swimming pool. If you play with one in the sea, connect a rope to it for someone on shore to hold. Never take an inflatable out in strong winds.

Calling the lifeguard

Thomas finds the lifeguard.
'Look, those children need help!'
The lifeguard has seen the children
too. He calls the beach rescue crew
patrolling the shore in their boat.

Calling 999

'What would I do if I couldn't find
a lifeguard?' Thomas asks.
'Find a telephone, dial 999
and ask for the coastguard,'
says the lifeguard.
'999 calls are free.
If someone is in
trouble by a river, ask
for an ambulance or
the police.'

SAFETY FACTS

If you are swept out to sea, keep hold of
anything that floats. Raise one arm to signal
for help and shout as loudly as you can.
Keep your head, and as much of your body
as possible, out of the water.

To the rescue

The patrol boat picks up the tired swimmers and speeds back to the beach.

'Could I rescue someone who fell off a jetty or a pier, or into a river?' asks Thomas.

'Never on your own,' says the lifeguard. 'You should think of your own safety first.'

Helping people in trouble

Do not go into the water unless you have been trained in life saving. Throw a lifebelt, a rope or anything that floats.

If someone is almost in reach, lie down and hold out a branch, a towel or clothes tied together to pull the person ashore. Ask someone else to hold on to you, so you do not fall in too.

SAFETY FACTS

Captain's orders

If you go out in a boat, *always* wear a life jacket and do what you are told.

At the harbour

Mum and Dad are proud of Thomas for his quick thinking. They decide to celebrate by going down to the harbour for some fish and chips.

By the quayside

There are all sorts of things to see from the quayside. Several fishing boats are lined up and a ferry is just leaving.

Currents

They watch a sailing boat scooting past in the breeze.

'Don't lean over too far,' says Mum, as the children peer over the barrier. 'That current is running very fast and there are no lifeguards here to save you if you fall in!'

DANGER
Strong Tides
Deep Water
Please do not climb over rails

Don't touch!

Never play with any containers, machinery or fishing equipment you see lying on a quayside. They might be dangerous.

Dad fetches the fish and chips and everyone tucks in. 'What a great way to end an exciting day,' says Oliver.

Glossary

Breakwater A barrier that breaks the force of the waves.

Canal An artificial waterway, built for shallow boats, called barges.

Cliff A high, steep rocky slope, often facing the sea.

Cramp A sudden tightening of muscles, which causes pain and may stop you moving or swimming properly.

Current Water flowing in one direction.

Headland A large piece of high land that sticks out into the sea.

Life jacket A jacket filled with air or a lightweight material that stops people from sinking if they fall into the water.

Lifebelt A large ring that floats in water. People in difficulties in the water can cling on to a lifebelt, while waiting to be rescued.

Lifeguard A specially trained person who works on a beach or at a swimming pool to make sure people in the water are safe. They try to rescue anyone in danger of drowning.

Lock A small section of a canal with gates at either end. The water level in a lock can be changed to allow boats to pass to a higher or lower part of the canal.

Patrol To go around an area looking out for trouble.

Promenade A place to walk beside the sea.

Quayside The edge of a harbour where ships are tied up for loading and unloading.

Shingle A huge mass of pebbles on a seashore or river bed.

Sunburn Redness of the skin caused by the sun.

Tide The regular rise and fall of the sea, usually twice a day.

Weir A place where the river bed drops suddenly.

Useful addresses and websites

Amateur Swimming Association
www.britishswimming.org
This is the national governing body for swimming, diving, water polo, open water and synchronised swimming.

British Waterways
www.britishwaterways.co.uk
This site reveals the hidden world of Britain's inland waterways network, showing how to find and enjoy them, how they are managed and how to get involved in their future conservation.

Child Accident Prevention Trust,
18-20 Farringdon Lane, London EC1R 3HA
www.capt.org.uk
Provides downloadable fact sheets on accidents to children including drowning accidents and bath water scalds.

Environment Agency
www.environment-agency.gov.uk
The Environment Agency's aim is to protect, improve and promote recreation on or near water.

Maritime Coastguard Association
www.mcga.gov.uk
An organisation committed to preventing loss of life, continuously improving maritime safety and protecting the marine environment: safer lives, safer ships, cleaner seas.

Qualification Curriculum Authority
www.nc.uk.net/safeswimming/index.html
Produced by the Department for Education & Skills, this website provides guidance and ideas for teachers to support their planning and teaching of swimming activities. It also provides Splash Zone - material related to water safety that is designed for pupils in schools to use.

Quarry Products Association 'Play Safe, Stay Safe'
www.qpa.org/sch_pla.htm
This website is for children and teachers and warns of the dangers of playing in quarries. It includes a free educational resource pack with activities.

Royal Society for the Protection of Accidents (RoSPA),
Edgbaston Park, 353 Bristol Road, Birmingham, B5 7ST
www.rospa.com
Provides information and resources about water and leisure safety.

Safety Street,
PO Box 2078, Reading, Berkshire RG30 3FF
www.safetystreet.org.uk
An interactive safety education site that gives information on safety at home, on the beach, on the road and in towns.

Streetwise Safety Centre,
Unit 1 Roundways, Elliott Road, Bournemouth BH11 8JJ
www.streetwise.org.uk
An interactive safety education site giving information about safety in the home, in cities and on the beach and the road.

Royal Life Saving Society (UK)
www.lifesavers.org.uk
The Royal Life Saving Society provides information on aspects of water safety and includes details of life saving courses.

Royal National Lifeboat Institution (RNLI)
www.beachsafety.org.uk
This charity saves lives at sea as well as providing a beach rescue service in south-west England. Visit this RNLI website for games and educational resources.

Surf Life Saving Association of Great Britain
www.lifeguards.org.uk/about.htm
An organisation that aims to provide a safe and enjoyable environment on British beaches.

Wired for Health
www.wiredforhealth.gov.uk
This series of health websites managed by the Health Development Agency on behalf of the Department of Health and the Department for Education and Skills offers resources and games for teachers, pupils and parents.

Wild Over Waterways (WOW)
www.wow4water.net
Games, activities and great things to do.

Note to parents and teachers
Every effort has been made by the Publishers to ensure that these websites are suitable for children; that they are of the highest educational value, and that they contain no inappropriate or offensive material. However, because of the nature of the Internet, it is impossible to guarantee that the contents of these sites will not be altered. We strongly advise that Internet access is supervised by a responsible adult.

Index

bath 9
boats 27

canals 10, 30
currents 13, 28

emergencies
  at the river 25, 26-27
  at the seaside 25, 26-27

flags, safety 22

ice 11
inflatables 24

kayaking 12

lakes 11
lifeguards
  at the beach 14, 22, 25, 30
  at the pool 4, 5, 7, 30
life jacket 12, 27, 30
life saving 27

mudflats 19

paddling pools 8
ponds 8

quarries 11

reservoirs 11
rivers
  currents 13, 30
  rescue 13, 25, 26-27
  water 13
  weirs 11, 30

seaside
  cliffs 20
  harbour 28
  litter 16
  quay 28
  rescue 25, 26-27
  rock pools 21
  shells 17
  sun 14-15
  tides 19, 21, 30
  waves 18
sun cream 15
swimming
  in rivers 13, 16
  in the pool 4-5
  in the sea 22-23
swimming pool
  badges 6
  diving 5
  lifeguards 4, 7, 30
  rescue 7
  running 4
  safety 5
  slides 7